Poems

To Rob Kendall, who encouraged me to write, and David Ward, who badgered me to stand up and read

Steve Turner

Poems

A LION BOOK

Published by
Lion Publishing Plc
Mayfield House, 256 Banbury Road,
Oxford OX2 7DH, England
www.lion-publishing.co.uk
ISBN 0 7459 4802 2

First edition 2002
10 9 8 7 6 5 4 3 2 1 0

A catalogue record for this book is available
from the British Library

Typeset in 10/13 Baskerville BT
Printed and bound in Great Britain
by Cox & Wyman Ltd, Reading

Contents

History Lesson

City Sunset

People Who Love

I Am On the Kids' Side

I Don't Believe in Air

Careful How You Pray

Who Made the World?

Index of First Lines

Introduction

This book contains a selection of my poems picked from seven books published over the past twenty-seven years. As my editor, Rebecca Winter, has organized them by theme rather than by year or collection, angry compositions from my youth sit opposite tender verse from my maturity, and emulations of Lennon and Ginsberg are mixed in with emulations of Milne and Stevenson. To help you in your journey through the book, I offer here a word of explanation as to how I wrote what I did and why.

My earliest writing was done as a pre-school child, when I would compose poems, letters, stories and sermons on rolls of lining paper. At the same time I was spending a lot of time listening to the radio because, in common with many British families of the 1950s, we had no television. These activities were to be the foundation of my future writing. The former introduced me to the pleasure of creating and the latter to the power of the spoken word.

During most of my early years I did more reading than writing and it wasn't until the age of fifteen, when the music of Bob Dylan, The Beatles and Simon and Garfunkel was coming to the fore, that my urge to create returned. At the time I would have regarded myself as someone who liked poetry, but I hadn't yet discovered poets who were dealing with contemporary issues in contemporary language. I tried to appreciate the work of the past poets collected in various 'golden treasuries' of verse but the outmoded vocabulary and the unrecognizable landscape proved to be an obstacle. This was partly why I responded so eagerly to the work of the new rock lyricists. They may not have been poets but their songs suggested the possibility of a poetry that could be written for the voice as well as the page and which could embrace neon signs and skyscrapers along with mountains and lakes.

I went to my first poetry reading on 5 November 1965 and started writing seriously later that month in a hardback notebook smothered in CND stickers. The reading was held in a pub near Liverpool Street Station in London, and it was significant not only in introducing me to 'live' poetry but to the work of the mystical poet William Blake. I think that it was reading, more than anything, which convinced me that I should write poetry and that poetry deserved to be heard by the same people who listened to rock music. I imagined that there were a lot of people like me who had the appetite for poetry but who never had it presented to them in an exciting or relevant way.

A brief summary of my involvement in poetry would be to say that I started in 1965 and never stopped. I realize now that many people start writing in their teens, maybe as a way of understanding the emotional turmoils of adolescence, but give up in their twenties, their work unseen by anyone else. The most significant factor in keeping me going was the discovery, in 1967, of a local poetry group which met fortnightly in the back room of a pub. The routine was that poets would read their work through the evening in the way that folk singers performed in folk clubs. I went along several times before I had the courage to perform my own work. I gave my first reading on 31 January 1968, and it provided a fresh sense of purpose. I not only had the critical comment of fellow poets but a specific audience to hold in mind as I wrote. It also increased my productivity. In order to appear at every meeting I had to write at least six poems a fortnight.

The earliest of these poems were conscious imitations of work I had liked. I had been moved in particular ways and I wanted to reproduce those effects in others. I still advise beginners to start by imitating, because you soon lose the obvious likenesses to those you admire and forge your own style out of a storehouse of poetic techniques.

In those early days I was influenced by photography, painting, films, cartoons, music and comedy, as well as by poetry. There was a feeling, in the late sixties, that all the popular arts were coming together and that barriers between 'high' art and 'low' art were coming down.

In 1969 Michael Horovitz edited *Children of Albion* for Penguin Books, a collection of so-called 'underground' poetry. In an accompanying essay he argued forcefully for the acceptance of a new oral poetry, the value of which wasn't dependent on academic post-mortems. He bemoaned the fact that poetry had become removed from its roots as a spoken art and divorced from the music and movement which the Greek poets used to accompany their performances. Like many others, he felt that the art of people like Bob Dylan had served as a reminder that poetry had become restrained by the invention of the printing press. Horovitz wasn't against printed poetry – indeed he edited his own magazine *New Departures* – but he wanted it to be the score for a performance. In common with most of the poets he published, he didn't want poetry to be produced only for a readership of fellow poets.

My first published poems appeared in small duplicated magazines which were sold to friends and workmates, but then I started sending work to general magazines. My first important publication was in *Honey*, a women's magazine of the time, which devoted a whole page to my work. I then had work published in the *Sunday Times*, *Cosmopolitan* and *Rolling Stone*.

I think it was Brian Patten who once said that his first collection of poems was 'a record of waking up' and that all his subsequent writing would deal with the process of trying to stay awake. The poems in my first published collection, *Tonight We Will Fake Love*, were written during a time when I studied theology briefly under Dr Francis Schaeffer at the L'Abri community in Switzerland, then left home and came to work in London. It really is a record of me waking up – to God, to relationships and to city life. I arrived in London during September 1970, and the bulk of the poems which ended up being collected for the first book were written between then and 1973, during which time I moved flat seven times, fell in and out of love more than once, suffered a broken engagement and worked for two years as a rock journalist.

Tonight We Will Fake Love was published in 1974 by Charisma Books, a division of Charisma Records, whose star bands at the time were Genesis and Van Der Graf Generator. To be published by Charisma was a fulfilment of my dream to see poetry marketed alongside rock music. I had seen a news item in *Melody Maker* announcing that Canadian singer/songwriter Leonard Cohen and Charisma Records owner Tony Stratton-Smith were combining forces to start a publishing company, in the belief that 'some of the best writing today is being done by what we might call rock writers'. I sent my manuscript of *Tonight We Will Fake Love* to them and, some months later, received a phone call from Stratton-Smith himself accepting me as one of their first authors.

When the book was published I was greeted by a lead review in the *Daily Mail*, written by literary editor Peter Lewis and headlined, 'At last, a poet who captures today with all the flair of a rock number.' I was pleased, not only because it was a significant and favourable review, but because it had commended me for doing exactly what I had set out to do.

Nice and Nasty, published in 1980, was my next collection, and it was an angrier book. The advent of punk rock had made me think about the role of subversion in art. I wondered how it was possible to engage readers, lull them into a sense of comfort, and then ultimately shock them by attacking their most cherished views. I admired the 1960s playwright Joe Orton for his ability to use farce to overturn the values normally held by middle-class theatre-goers. I enjoyed Orton's impishness and his tightly sprung lines, which could simultaneously engage and disarm. By calling my book *Nice and Nasty* I was trying to imply this dual function – not some nice poems and some nasty poems, but a smile and a stab at the same time.

Many of the poems from this period remain significant to me. 'Christmas is Really for the Children', which takes the popular parental refrain to expose our ignorance of Easter, has become my most anthologized poem. 'Five Hundred Million Pounds', written after seeing a captioned photograph of the then Earl of Grosvenor (now Duke of Westminster) with his new wife at Heathrow airport on their way to a honeymoon in Hawaii, is one of my personal favourites. 'Creed' was written after I read an interview with comedian Peter Cook, in which he said that satire was dead because there were no longer any sacred cows left to demolish. I could see that while the old sacred cows – the church, marital fidelity and the class system – which much of the satire of his generation had picked on, were now disappearing, new sacred cows had be put in their place.

I was by this time travelling quite widely to read my poems. I had done two tours of America where I'd read at colleges, coffee bars and theatres in an arc reaching up from Washington DC and New York, through Chicago and

Minneapolis and down into California. I had also been to Russia, where I was fortunate enough to read to a group of refusenik writers. I had long had respect for writers such as Yevtushenko and Voznesensky and knew that poetry was highly valued in Russian culture. I was touched when after a reading one of the writers said to me, through a translator, 'You are from London but you are a Leningrad man.'

In California I did some of my first recordings of poetry and music. I had become friendly with producer/ singer/songwriter T-Bone Burnett, and he suggested we went into the studio and experimented with some poems. We worked on three poems from *Nice and Nasty* – 'Stuck at Seventeen', 'Houses Without Faces' and 'Religion is the Opium of the People'. T-Bone produced and played rhythm guitar, David Mansfield played lead guitar and Jerry Scheff played stand-up bass. I was fortunate to have such accomplished musicians – David had played on a recording with Allen Ginsberg, Jerry (ex-Elvis Presley band) had played with Jim Morrison of The Doors, and T-Bone had played on Bob Dylan's Rolling Thunder Tour.

Up to Date, a volume of earlier work and some new poems was published in 1983. My ventures into music studios were reflected in a lot of the new poems in that collection. 'Assassin', 'The City Without Love' and 'The Prophet' were, for example, all written to be recorded with a musical backing.

Looking back on my fourth collection, *The King of Twist*, published in 1992, I can now see the seeds of the poetry that was to follow. Technically I was becoming increasingly attracted to rhyme ('The Jogger's Prayer', 'Armageddon in Green', 'I Wish I Could Believe') and at the same time I was now the father of two primary-school-age children and was tuning in to their lives and thoughts ('Questions', 'Rebecca's Father').

Having my own children re-introduced me to children's literature. I re-read authors like A.A. Milne and Robert Louis Stevenson and read Roald Dahl and Michael Rosen for the first time. Some of the poets who had been an inspiration to me in my teens, like Roger McGough and Brian Patten, were now writing for children, and this encouraged me to think that this was the next logical step for me.

Writing for children, principally, I imagined, for the seven to eleven age group, brought back all of the excitement and challenge of my first years of writing. Unlike adults, children don't pretend to 'appreciate' poetry. They have no idea of what they 'should' like but they'll respond with enthusiasm to what gets through to them. They are a great audience and visiting them in schools and book shops has helped keep the typical reader very firmly in my mind.

My collections for children have been based on themes because I now need to set myself a challenge rather than wait for inspiration to strike seventy-two times in a relatively short period. For my first collection for children, *The Day I Fell Down the Toilet*, published in 1996, the themes were to do with poetry itself – language, rhyme, metaphor, memory, message, for instance. For my second collection, *Dad, You're Not Funny*, published in 1999, the themes were picked from the story of my childhood, such as friends, games, places, animals and dreams. For my most recent children's book, *The Moon Has Got His Pants On*, published in 2001, I wrote three poems for every hour of a typical day in a child's life.

I'm often asked if I still write 'adult' poetry and the answer is that I haven't had time. I've published more poems in the past five years than I did in the twenty-five years before *The Day I Fell Down the Toilet* and have sold more books. Even though poetry written for children may appear easy because the construction is not complex and the vocabulary is basic, I can vouch for the fact that it is not easy to write. It is, however, enjoyable to write, and I think that overall it has given me more personal satisfaction than any other writing I have done.

It was an interesting experience for me to read through the selection that Rebecca had made. My more recent poems seemed more carefree and optimistic and the range of subjects a lot broader. I could see the technical imperfections in the earlier work and the times when I had strained for an effect. Some of these we took out because they hadn't stood the test of time. Some needed minor tinkering to make them roadworthy. Others remain as they were first published because I know that they have become favourites, and it's best not to attempt to improve a favourite.

Steve Turner
London, 2002

Inside My Head

Inside My Head

Inside my head there's a forest,
A castle, a cottage, a king,
A rose, a thorn, some golden hair,
A turret, a tower, a ring.

A horse, a prince, a secret word,
A giant, a gaol, a pond,
A witch, a snake, a bubbling pot,
A wizard, a warlock, a wand.

Inside my head there's an ocean,
A parrot, a pirate, a gull,
A cave, a sword, a silver coin,
A princess, an island, a skull.

A ghost, a ghoul, a creaking stair,
A shadow, a shudder, a shout,
A flame, a grave, a swirling mist,
A rainbow, an angel, a cloud.

Inside my head there's a country
Of mountains and valleys and streams,
It all comes alive when I listen
To stories, to poems, to dreams.

A Way With Words

Had a way with words.
Seduced them from the hemispheres,
had them falling at his lips.
Had a way with women.
Breathed life into their shapes,
understood their hidden meanings.
And the words
worked on the women
and the women
formed the words.
He had a way with
women and words,
words and women,
although words never failed him.

In My World

In my world
I would write
of golden suns
if it weren't
for the obscuring clouds.
I would write
of the wind-bent grass
but all the fields
are tarmacked
& multistorey.
Instead I'll be
an urban Wordsworth
writing of
reinforced concrete landscapes
& clear brown skies
where
to wander lonely as a cloud
is just not advisable
after dark.

Short Poem

Short poems
are fun.
You can see
at a glance
whether you
like them
or not.

Depression

Came here
to write
a poem
on depression
but

got fed up
and left.

I Like Words

I like words.
Do you like words?
Words aren't hard to find:
Words on walls and words in books,
Words deep in your mind.

Words in jokes
That make you laugh,
Words that seem to smell.
Words that end up inside out,
Words you cannot spell.

Words that fly
And words that crawl,
Words that screech and bump.
Words that glide and words that swing,
Words that bounce and jump.

Words that paint
And words that draw,
Words that make you grin.
Words that make you shake and sweat,
Words that touch your skin.

Words of love
That keep you warm,
Words that make you glad.
Words that hit you, words that hurt,
Words that make you sad.

Words in French
And words in slang,
Words like 'guy' and 'dude'.
Words you make up, words you steal,
Words they say are rude.

I like words.
Do you like words?
Words come out and play.
Words are free and words are friends,
Words are great to say.

Careful

Be careful
or the poet man
will come and
turn you into
the poem
he's just
writi

Something I've Never Said Before

I'm running short
of things I've never said
to anyone before.

It began with lines
borrowed from screenplays
and whispered in dark back rows.
Then I invented
a few of my own
making them more potent
when the effects wore off.

It's many love poems later
and I'm low on originals.
There have been too many
only girls in the world,
too many confessions
meant at the time.

For you I had wanted
something new and unreleased.
You deserved at least that.
Instead you must take this.
It is something
I have never said
to anyone before.

If Words Were Birds

If words
were birds
sentences
would fly
in formation
across page-white
skies.
Dictionaries would
have bars,
      speeches
would darken
the sun.
If words
were birds
fly formation

                sentences

                      skies across

                  page white dictionaries.

                        Bars

              would have speeches.

                        Blacken the

              would

                      sun.

Write a Poem About Anything

Write a poem about anything
My mind goes blank
No film in my projector
No fuel in my tank.

I look into the atmosphere
Doodle on a page
Write my name in capitals
Add my class and age.

The more I try to think of things
The less I think I think
My skull is overheating
My brain is on the blink.

Then these words come cranking out
Splutter, clink, clank:
'Write a poem about anything
My mind goes blank...'

The Portrait of the Artist

I was deprived.
I never had the unhappy childhood
necessary for greatness.
The worst things that happened
were shopping at weekends,
unfinished homework,
and the ghost beneath the bed.
My one regret in life:
that I was not born
on the bad side of town.
At fourteen I wanted to be
Heavyweight Champion Of The World
but I was seventy pounds too light
and had no criminal record.
I could've been the next John Lennon
but my parents couldn't misunderstand me.
My first novel dried up
through lack of trauma;
no skeletons in my cupboards;
no ghosts to exorcise.
Now I'm going to be a poet.
I'm looking for the mess
that could be the key,
the chip that could be the spur.
If only things had been different.
If only I could have been like the rest.
All I asked of life was
some poverty to flee from
and a pit to climb out of.

Secrets

I wrote a secret message
In lines of secret ink
So no one could discover
The secret words I think.

I took the secret message
When no one else was in
And secretly I hid it
Inside my secret tin.

I found a secret tree-trunk
Which held a secret fold
And slipped my secret package
Deep in the secret hole.

When I had grown much older
I sought the secret tree
To see if I could find the tin
Which held the secret me.

But all the trees looked taller
And changed a lot somehow.
They looked at me as if to say,
'Your secret's secret now.'

Tongue

The tongue
is where
the mind
comes out
into the open.

Lips move
so to speak.

The tongue
is where
the mind
comes out
into the open.

Mind
what you say.

Sticks and Stones

Sticks and stones
only break your bones,
but words
can tear your heart out.

Dial-a-Poem is Temporarily Out of Order

All poems have been cancelled today
because of the national poetry strike.
Poets are demanding equal rights
with rock stars and saints.
They want
to be
paid by the
column inch
rather than
the
word.
They want overtime rates for
nocturnal inspiration,
danger money for love affairs that end.
Poets are demanding a closed shop.
Rhymsters and graffiti artists
will not be admitted,
nor any employee of Hallmark Cards.
Poets want pens that don't run in your pocket.
Poets want bigger cigarette packets for epic verse.
Poets want repeat fees for every line memorized.
Poets want better thinking conditions.
All poems have been cancelled today.
Pens and keyboards lie idle.
The general public are advised
to stock up with alternative forms of literature.
All poems have been cancelled.
No one notices the sun rise,
no one hears the wind.
Somewhere a poet falls in love
but he can't put it into words.

The Last Word

You always think you're right.
I always think I'm right.
You think I'm wrong
to think I'm right.
I think you're wrong
to think you're right.
We can't both be right.
You want the last word.
I want the last word.
When you say,
'You want the last word,'
you hope that will be the last word.
When I say,
'You say I want the last word
because you want the last word,'
you say,
'There you go again –
you're having the last word.'
'No, no, no,' I say.
'There you are,' you say,
'last word again.'
You think you're right.
I think I'm right,
You think I'm wrong
to think I'm right,
I think you're wrong
to think you're right.

Who Am I?

Who Am I?

I'm boy and child and brother and son
Him over there, the poetry one
Passport holder 41604
I'm all of these things, and much much more.

I'm legs and arms and body and head
A weight that makes a dip in the bed
A size that stands in front of your door
I'm all of these things, and much much more.

I'm skin and bone and muscle and brain
A pumping heart, a feeler of pain
A bundle of cells with ME at the core
I'm all of these things, and much much more.

I'm every thought that rises and falls
The face that stares from mirrors on walls
A secret code passed down from before
I'm all of these things, and much much more.

Birth

I didn't ask
to be born.
I wasn't even
there to ask.
When you are born
you can ask for
anything.
Almost anything.
You cannot ask
to be unborn.
If you do
there is very little
that can be done.
I didn't ask
to be born.
I was under age
at the time.
My parents had
to decide
on my behalf.
I'm glad that
I was born.
You have to be born
to be glad.

Who Was I Before I Was Born?

You were a song
that had yet to be sung,
You were a word
on the tip of a tongue,
You were a plan
chalked up on a board,
You were a gleam
in the eye of the Lord.

For Lianne, Aged One

As far as is possible, stay as you are,
with the eye clear and open
and washed clean of fear;
with the skin untracked
by the sad workings of the heart,
lips unskilled in spite.
As far as is possible, stay as you are,
the morning's first light
cause enough for joy,
each passing face
judged only by the colour of its smile.
As far as is possible, stay as you are.
Gaze out at the world
with its mystery and noise,
but refuse all offers to join.
Be backwards in evil,
advanced in love.
As far as is possible, stay as you are,
with the upturned face
and the open palm,
with the stumble of faith
and the shout of hope.
For of such is the Kingdom.

As You Learn

Just as you learn to climb,
The ladder snaps its rungs.
Just as you like yourself,
The self you like has gone.
Just as you learn to love,
True love has passed you by.
Just as you learn to live,
You have to learn

Blood, Sweat and Tears

My blood knows where to go,
perspiration knows when to begin,
tears fall on cue.

If I were my blood
I'd take time off
every now and then,
take wrong turnings,
misinterpret instructions.

If I were perspiration
I'd arrive too soon,
hang around too long
and disappear when needed.

And if I were my tears
I'd forget to stock up,
I'd get low on salt
and leave without asking.

My body's in good shape.
It's upstanding and reliable.
We have so little in common.

Nothing

What are you doing? Nothing.
And this time the answer is true.
I sit here doing nothing
because there is nothing to do.

I hold my head in my hands
I stare very hard into space
I swing my legs to and fro
and pick at a spot on my face.

How wonderful is nothing,
a subject that has no exam,
a time when, instead of 'I do',
I can simply say that 'I am'.

Life Begins at Forty and Closes Early

i Ageing

At some point in his life
there came a shortage
of future.
At some point in his life
the past became more certain,
more reliable.
It was then they called him old.
It was then they bought him
a wooden chair to live in
and a window to look out of.
When he became hungry
he thought of meals
he'd once eaten.
When he was lonely
he imagined a friend.
When he was depressed
he remembered an adventure.

He lived in his chair
and grew fat on the past.

ii Remembering

Although
    he liked to remember
he did not
    like to remember
that he was old.

iii Wondering

One day
he wondered whether
his years of living
had been only to provide
some food for thought.
Food to be eaten now
in this chair
by a window.

He wondered that;
and it became further
food for thought.

iv Sleeping

There's a sleep
that has a pillow,
two white sheets,
a blanket
and a beginning.

He dreamed
of that sleep
when there were
no good memories
to look forward to.

v Nothing

After breathing
is over and done with
he knew there would be

something
    or nothing.
He had always thought
that there was something
quite frightening
about something.
Now he knew
there could be nothing
more frightening than nothing.

vi Showing

From his chair
by a window
he showed me
the maps on his face.
He showed me
where the lines
would form, how
my flesh would hang
in years to come.
He'd been around
the corner of the
last ambition
this side of silence.
He was hoping that
God believed in him
in a deeper way
than he had believed
in God.

Then he went on
living in his chair
and growing fat on the past.

The Mirror

Whenever I look in the mirror
I find that it's me who is there,
Wearing identical clothing
And staring straight into my stare.

I've tried creeping up without warning
And peeking from outside the frame.
But whatever I look like that day
Looks back – it's exactly the same.

I think, can I trick my reflection
And glimpse someone famous or rich?
A model or maybe a film star,
I really don't mind what or which.

Yet it's me who gets in the picture,
Always me in the glass gazing out;
Sleepy, untidy or grumpy.
But me. Absolutely. No doubt.

Backwards

I came into this world
at the age of eighty-one.
At seventy-eight I started school,
leaving for university
when I was just sixty-three.
I took my first job at sixty,
married at forty-five
and had two children.
I retired when I was twenty
so that I could spend
more time on my hobbies
and at ten I was put into
a young people's home.
At five I started forgetting things,
falling over and spilling my food.
At two I lost my voice.
By the time I was one
I could hardly walk
and had to be pushed around
in a chair with wheels.
In the end I was spending
most of my time in bed,
dribbling and sleeping,
crying in the night,
waiting to be born.

How Fitting
(Joseph Martin, 1883–1978)

How fitting
to become a child
before this leap
into eternity.
How fitting
that at this end
it is so much like
the beginning.
Again they bring
you food and wipe
away the traces.
Again a walk
from chair to door
seems like a journey,
buttons are hard work,
dressing is an art.
How fitting
that this largest part
of eternity
should take you
as a child.

Old Soldier

(Joseph Martin, 1883–1978)

I am bent and creased
although I never liked
things bent or creased.
The years, they have
untidied me.
My skin has
become one size too large,
like a shirt I would return.
My bones have shrunk
inside me
as if exposed to the weather.
The years, they have got it in
for old soldiers.
They snipe at our pride.
Can't go on parade like this.
Have to sit it out
in the barrack room.
Have to sit it out in the chair.

Nobody Likes You When You Grow Up

Nobody likes you when you grow up.
Nobody offers to steady your cup,
Feeds you food on the end of a fork
Or thinks that you're great for learning to walk.

Nobody holds your hand on the stair
Or whips out a comb to tidy your hair,
Rubs your face to get rid of the dirt,
Kisses you better whenever you're hurt.

Nobody sings you songs in the dark,
Carries you home after games in the park,
Strokes your forehead and tickles your chin,
Praises the width of your mischievous grin.

When things you touch just happen to break,
Nobody says, 'It was just a mistake.
Oh, whoops-a-daisy! We'll pick it up.'
No, nobody likes you when you grow up.

A Few Thousand Days

One day the world
will carry on without me
just as it did
for the few thousand years
until I was born.
I'd like to imagine
windows breaking of their own accord
on that day,
swollen-eyed multitudes
pacing the streets,
a grey mist visiting the city,
everything somehow different,
incomplete.
But almost one hundred per cent
of the world
won't notice this new silence.
They will drink coffee
and change trains
unaware that mankind
has been reshaped,
unaware that a few thousand days
just seeped through a hole
two seconds wide.

Natural History

Most of us
do not go down
in history,
we just go down.
Our versions of
how things happened
perish behind our eyes.
Then our witnesses follow,
until the tip
of the last tongue
we could be upon
is swollen silent.
Years later,
children kicking leaves
in some churchyard
will subtract birthdays from deathdays
and laugh at old-fashioned names
such as Stephen.

Heaven

What happens in heaven?
Will I sit on a cloud?
Is walking or talking
Or jumping allowed?

Will I be on my own
Or with some of my friends?
Does it go on for ever
Or eventually end?

What happens in heaven?
Will I play a harp's strings?
I can't play piano
I can't even sing.

Who chooses the music
That angels inspire?
Who does the auditions
For the heavenly choir?

What happens in heaven?
Are the streets paved with gold?
Is it crowded with people
Who're incredibly old?

Will I know who I am?
Will I know what I'm called?
If I pinch myself hard
Will I feel it at all?

What happens in heaven?
Do I go through a gate?
What if I get myself lost
Or turn up too late?

Is my name on a list?
Is the gatekeeper nice?
Can you sneak in for nothing
Or is there a price?

In Heaven

In heaven there will be no policemen,
because there will be no crime.
There will be no soldiers,
because there will be no war.
There will be no doctors,
no surgeons, no nurses.
There will be no prison warders,
security guards, undertakers,
insurance salesmen, judges,
watch-makers, fire-fighters, evangelists,
gossip columnists, prostitutes
or ambulance drivers.
But there will be poets.
Poets and musicians.
This much we know.

History Lesson

History Lesson

History repeats itself.
Has to.
No one listens.

Who Made a Mess?

Who made a mess of the planet
And what's that bad smell in the breeze?
Who punched a hole in the ozone
And who took an axe to my trees?

Who sprayed the garden with poison
While trying to scare off a fly?
Who streaked the water with oil slicks
And who let my fish choke and die?

Who tossed that junk in the river
And who stained the fresh air with fumes?
Who tore the fields with a digger
And who blocked my favourite views?

Who's going to tidy up later
And who's going to find what you've lost?
Who's going to say that they're sorry
And who's going to carry the cost?

Words and Deeds

I know.
And it's easy to know.
Opinions keep the mind
    well dressed.
Actions are where
the problems begin.
There's always the mortgage,
a meeting, a reputation...
Truth could be
such a beautiful thing,
if only one had the time.

Gun

What is a gun for?
A gun is for making things.
What does it make?
Orphans, widows,
    grief...

Unknown Soldier

Was he old?
No, not old.
Twenty or so,
no more.
An officer?
A private,
no stripes,
front line.
Decorations?
Stone over
his body,
medal for
his mother.
Was he famous?
No,
but he went at
the bidding
of the famous.
What do
the records say?
Only
that his records
were lost
in the world's next war.

Remembrance Sunday

At the going
down of the sun
and in the morning
we do our best
to remember them,
from comic books
and photographs
and films with Jack Hawkins.

At the rising
of the moon
and in the evening,
black and white
memories slip away
like soldiers that

    stop

        writing

           home.

Can Hate Come Home?

Can Hate come home to play, mother,
For Hate is daring and fierce?
I'd rather you played with Love, my child,
For Love has a sister called Peace.

Can Pride come home to play, mother,
For Pride is clever and cool?
I'd rather you played with Humility,
For Pride can lead to a fall.

Can Lies come home to play, mother,
For Lies can duck and can dive?
I'd rather you played with Truth, my child,
For Truth has nothing to hide.

Can Greed come home to play, mother,
For Greed has so many toys?
I'd rather you played with Contentment,
For Contentment has far deeper joys.

Assassin

The assassin was
a most ordinary man.
Ask his teacher.
Ask his mother.
Ask his girlfriend.
Ask the doorman.
And it was on
a most ordinary day
that he slid the bolt
that slid the metal
through the cloth
and through the skin.
It felt most ordinary.
Almost no effort.
As easy as blinking.
And when they led him
to the cellroom
he felt ordinary.
He felt hungry.
This did not feel like history.
This did not feel like news.
This did not feel like
the end of an era.

Murder

They called
him
a murderer
but I thought
he was simply
breath   taking.

In the Interests of National Security

It is wrong
to be wrong
unless
you are wrong
while protecting
the right people
from wrong.
Then it is
all right to be wrong
because rulers
have the rights
on what is right
and there's no one
big enough
to tell a ruler
what is wrong.
Right?

(Wrong)

High-Fibre Massacre

We were speaking one evening
about the importance of a high-fibre diet
when a woman butted in
from behind the television screen,
saying that her husband and children
had been slaughtered in Beirut:
and she was crying and I was thinking,
I'm glad I'm not that woman.
I'm glad I'm not her husband.
I'm glad I'm not her children.
Someone in the *Sunday Times*
claims that dieting can make you fat,
and we carried on discussing
how this could be possible,
and talked of polyunsaturated fats
and other poly-things
until I was distracted
by the voice of an old man saying
that his grandchildren and his son
had been massacred.
He was not crying, and I wondered why.
He had a grey beard and a small knitted hat.
He took a walking stick
and pointed to their bloodstains on a white wall.
Still he did not cry.
I remember thinking that I would have cried.

A caption came up:
THEY TOOK MY SON,
KILLED HIM WITH AN AXE
AND THREW HIM OVER THAT WALL.

Though dieting can make you fat,
exercise can make you thin.
But, it must be noted,
squash and tennis are anaerobic –
according to the *Sunday Times* –
and it's far better to swim, walk or run.
No body wants to be a fat body.
The woman in a country far away
wanted to know why God had left her alone
to look after her children.
Why wasn't she left a man?
She cannot look for work with all her children.
The bodies were dragged into a deep trench,
powdered with lime, and bulldozed over with earth.
The woman, she cried on to our carpet.
When I think of her grief,
I think of exercise and margarine,
of sacrifice and loss.

Lord, Lord

You were hungry
and I was sorry.
You were thirsty
and I blamed the world.
You were a stranger
and I pointed you out.
You were naked
and I turned you in.
You were sick
and I said a prayer.
You were in prison
and I wrote a poem.

In the End

In the end.
In the very end of the last moment,
when the smoking stub of the world
is completely shadowed by a descending
heel, we'll call in the experts
for their considered opinion.
We'll arrange for an apocalyptic
edition of *Time* magazine,
complete with artists' impressions.
We'll comfort ourselves with the fact
that it has never happened before.
In the end, we'll be deciding
whether to decide.
In the very end of the last moment,
we'll falter,
half-believing,
crushed.

Armageddon in Green

'British soldiers have completed "environmentally
friendly" military exercises in West Germany.'
The Times, 26 September 1989

How would you like your war, madam?
And how would you like it, sir?
Would you like a new explosive
That doesn't pollute the air?
Oh, we've found a way of fighting
I think you're going to love,
It's modern but it's sensitive,
It'll fit you like a glove.

We'll be fighting
For our country and our Queen,
But this time round
We're going to make it green.
We'll crawl like snakes
On our hands and on our knees.
We'll shoot to kill
But we'll never bruise the trees.

Would you like to see a bullet
That's completely free of lead,
And a caring sort of army
That cremates you when you're dead?
Would you like to see a cannon
That recycles all its shells,
And a soundproof rocket launcher
That can heat a house as well?

We'll be fighting
For our country and our Queen,
But this time round
We're going to make it green.
We'll blind and maim
But we'll do it all in love.
We'll drop our bombs
But we'll always pick them up.

Our uniforms are camouflaged,
You'd think we were slabs of turf.
We decorate our hats with twigs
Out of friendship for the earth.
We like to spend our fighting days
Out in the open air.
We take the mud and rub it in
Our faces and on our hair.

We're fighting
For our country and our Queen,
But this time round
We're going to make it green.
Be nice to hedgerows
By shooting over the tops.
Mind that rabbit!
Don't walk all over the crops!

If we come across a village
And we frizzle it to the ground,
We'll dig the ashes in the soil
Then scatter some seeds around.
For a loss of population
Is good news for grass and plants.
The forests of the Amazon
Could flourish again in France.

We're fighting
For our country and our Queen,
But this time round
We're going to make it green.
Help save the world,
Keep people out of the way.
Humans come and go,
But the planet, it's got to stay.

Make Me Poet Laureate

Make me poet laureate
For the world that writhes in pain
For the child sucked from the womb
For the prisoner in chains

For those who die in thousands
While the rich sort out their scores
For the unknown disappeared
In those boring foreign wars.

Make me poet laureate
For the stranger in the land
For the daughter who is raped
At her father's evil hand

For the runaway who sleeps
On a mattress made of stone
For the worker out of work
Left to waste away at home.

Make me poet laureate
For the victims no one hears
For every child that's battered
While its screams are gagged with fear

For those too weak to argue
For those who have no tongue
For those too old to matter
In a world which loves the young.

Make me poet laureate
For the beggar at the gate
For those who cry for justice
But are told they have to wait

Not for presidents and queens
Who are overwhelmed by choice,
But for those whose mouths are stopped –
And so can't afford a voice.

City Sunset

City Sunset (i)

On a freshly
laid blue sky
drips the brok
en yolk of sun
light.
Soon darkness
ambles on and
wipes
away the traces.

City Sunset (ii)

Tall buildings
poised
like chessmen
in cloudy fingers.
Sneaky old sun
makes
a last move.

The City Without Love

In the city without love
buildings turn their backs on you,
the night air hangs around
like an enemy in waiting.
You hope you will not fall sick
in the city without love
because the mortician
is nearer than the surgeon
and the citizens are lazy.
You are from the bad side of the family,
your words come out as nonsense,
your questions are annoying,
in the city without love.
In the city without love
you are walking on the wrong street
at the wrong time of night.
This is where the rough boys live,
this is the haunted room,
this is where the strangers stare,
this is the city without love.

Untitled

We say there is no God
    (quite easily)
when amongst the curving
steel and glass of our own
    proud creations.

They will not argue.

Once we were told of a
    heaven
but the last time we strained
    to look up
we could see only skyscrapers
shaking their heads
    and smiling no.

The pavement is reality.

We say there is no God
    (quite easily)
when walking back through
Man's concrete achievements
but on reaching the park
our attention is distracted
by anthems of birds coming
from the greenery.
We find ourselves shouting
a little louder now because
    of the rushing streams.
Our voices are rained upon by
    the falling of leaves.

We should not take our arguments
    for walks like this.
The park has absolutely no manners.

Daily London Recipe

Take any number of them
you can think of,
pour into empty red bus
    until full,
and then push in
    ten more.
Allow enough time
to get hot under the collar
before transferring into
multistorey building.
Leave for eight hours,
and pour back into same bus
    already half full.
    Scrape remainder off.
When settled down
tip into terraced houses each
carefully lined with copy
of *Evening Standard* and *Tit Bits*.
Place mixture before open
television screen at 7 p.m.
and then allow to cool
in bed at 10:30 p.m.
May be served with
working overalls
or pinstripe suit.

Typical

You should have seen him.
Small as a child,
bent with age,
teetering through lunch crowds
in a ripped and greased raincoat.

You should have seen his face.
Deserted and ruined,
overgrown with stubble,
tumbling towards the earth.

There must have been a last embrace.
It coils inside him now,
a pain both dull and warm.
He has not outgrown the need for touch.
He has not gone blind to beauty.

You should have seen the crowds.
They walked around him
as if he were a mess;
as if he were a stain, a smell,
a death, an accident.

You should have seen me.
I did the same,
all the time wondering
what society should do.

Inside my upright body
beats a beggar of a heart;
a mess, a stain, a smell,
a death. No accident.

It Must Be Hard

It must be hard for those
whose faces make children cry,
whose voices make adults embarrassed,
whose skin turns our eyes to lovelier things.
They must get used to silence.
They must think of humans
as those who turn away,
who withdraw their smiles and sounds
like hands from an angry dog.
There is nothing as evil to us as ugliness.
It deserves only a room to hide itself in,
some air, and a little light.
Meanwhile, we help by telling
children not to stare
and by keeping the jokes to ourselves.

Houses Without Faces

Houses without faces
House without faces
Boarded up eyes
Corrugated teeth
Houses without faces
Houses without faces
You can do so much
When you haven't got a face
You can hide so much
When you haven't got a face
Houses without faces
Houses without faces
Boarded up eyes
Corrugated teeth
People without faces
Faces without people
Boarded up people
Corrugated people
Burned out people
Masked up people
People without faces
Houses without people
Houses with people
People without houses
People without houses
Burned out of their houses
Burned out terraced houses
Houses without faces
Houses without faces

To Those I Will Never Meet

She
sits over there
on the bus
on the train
on the tube.
She
makes reading
the *Evening Standard*
a difficult task.
She
is aware that I am
reading in between the lines
and far beyond the margins.
She
adjusts herself
for better presentation.
I gain an interest
in No Smoking signs
and obscure shadows
in the window.
Obstructing the doors
causes delay and can
be dangerous.
A station foreman
can earn up to £X.40
– more with overtime.
She
notices my noticing.
I give her profile left
– a good one.
My attitude – disinterested,
harder to catch than

most men.
Do you? How far have?
What is your? Have you?
... ever wished
introductions weren't needed?
Our gazes meet like
billiard balls... that fall
into opposite pockets.
The best jobs are always
to be found in
the *Evening News*.
Wimbledon got off
to a good start.
A girl on the tube
on the train
on the bus
got off at Golders Green.
She left me wondering,
whether I left her wondering,
a poem like this,
about me.

Stranger

I feel strange
to be your stranger.
Mid-morning lone ranger.
Daylight danger.

Do not accept
any sweets I may offer.
Do not talk to me.
Beware of me.
Tell mummy
about the funny man
that smiled.
I am the sort that lurks
in shop doorways
when only other people
go out.
I act suspiciously
I am not to be trusted.

Every criminal
you will ever read about
will be a stranger.
(They were strangers
said a neighbour yesterday.
The garden was overgrown.
We never had anything to
do with them.)
Strangers throw up
on the last train home
at night.

They sit right next to you
when there are two empty
seats in front.
They talk to themselves
in crowded streets.
No one really knows
that much about them.

You do not know
that much about me.
That is why, today,
I have become your stranger.
And because I am a stranger
you will not try and know
that much about me.

It's strange
being a stranger.
There seems little chance
of breaking out.
Or if I was to,
it would only confirm
my strangeness.

One Pair of Shoes

She has only one pair of shoes.
The shoes are torn.
Because the shoes are torn
she cannot go out.
Because she cannot go out
she has no friends.
Because she has no friends
she has no respect.
Because she has no respect
she is depressed.
Because she is depressed
she is angry.
Because she is angry
he beats her.
Because he beats her
she cannot go for work.
Because she cannot go for work
she has no money.
Because she has no money
she has only one pair of shoes.
And the shoes are torn.
The shoes are torn.

Back-Garden Poems

Eleven

A robin
stands on
frosted grass.
I accuse it
of cheap sentiment.

Eleven Thirty

Sheets have a great time
on the washing line.
Tired of lying down
in bed all day,
they really get loose.
They let it all hang out.
They shake their stuff.
Socks are more casual.
They've been around a bit.
Seen a lot of shoes.
Seen a lot of heels.
They flick their toes
and look vaguely bored.

Twelve Twenty

Sky looks angry.
Trees bristle.
Flowers shake.
Lawn gets ready
for another deluge.

One Thirty

Birds make bare trees
look like sheet music.
I try to whistle
an oak full of sparrows,
but they hop out of tune.

Three Forty-Five

The sun
is spilling
on roof tops.
The moon
wears an apron
and carries
a cloth.

Five Thirty

Not enough light
for part-time
nature poets.

Please Stand on the Right

Shepherd Street W.1. RDP 282M OPEN
Antiques PARK Plumes Piccadilly W.1.
IN IN   OUT OUT
Third Church of Christ The Scientist
Curzon Street   Daska   Sautters   Pipes
Lebanon   Libyan Arab Airlines
Keep Britain Tidy   Keep Britain Tidy
Aphrodites   Clarges   Look Left
Look Left   TMG 374M   Bolton Street
DOG FOULS FOOTWAY   FINE   £20
Evening Standard On Sale Here
Midland Bank   UNDERGROUND
TICKETS and TRAINS   No Entry
This machine is temporarily out of order
This machine is temporarily out of order
This machine is temporarily out of order.
TICKETS   IN   IN   IN   Victoria Line
Yellow Tickets   Take Ticket Here
The Comeback   The Goodbye Girl
PLEASE STAND ON THE RIGHT
Eminently Male   Oldham   I'd be lost without it.
Pregnant. Terrific! Brilliant!
Where can you go for a walk? Spend more time
in the open. Well they said it couldn't happen.
PLEASE STAND ON THE RIGHT.
Lost   London's greatest first class   To stop
escalator PUSH   I'd be lost without it
PLEASE STAND ON THE RIGHT
For those who prefer breast shaped bald facts
Madam Tussauds a nice person abortion help?
PLEASE STAND ON THE RIGHT
Two new London Transport Books Jack Jones

Portrait of A Man
PLEASE STAND ON THE RIGHT
Victoria Line Northbound
No Smoking   No Smoking   No Smoking
Private. Keep the doorway clear.
Green Park
Green Park   Green Park
Green Park   Green Park   Green Park
Green Park   Green Park   Green Park   Green Park.

Jubilee Road

I don't like going
Down Jubilee Road
Because Jubilee Road is rough.
The gardens are covered
In thistles and thorns
And motor-car parts and stuff.

I'd get home much quicker
Down Jubilee Road
But the big kids stand there and stare.
I could be kidnapped
On Jubilee Road
And no one down there would care.

Killing Time

Some people haven't got the time;
time to have time.
But we've got the time.
It's on our hands.
Our hands are empty.

Hands of the clock.
Clocking this. Clocking that.
Crawling the streets.
Creeping like a clock hand.
Hand me the bottle.
Hand me a glass.
Kill me some time.

Our glasses are empty.
Time, gentlemen, please.
Just looking! Sorry.
Just looking sorry.
It's nothing past nothing.
It's time to do nothing.

Doing time for killing time.
Crime on our hands.
Our clocks are empty.
Our streets are sorry.
Our time is dead.

British Rail Regrets

British Rail regrets
having to regret.
British Rail regrets
it cannot spell.
British Rail regrets
the chalk ran out.
British Rail regrets
that due to a staff shortage
there will be no one
to offer regrets.
British Rail regrets,
but will not be sending
flowers or tributes.
British Rail regrets
the early arrival
of your train.
This was due to industrious action.
British Rail regrets
that because of a work-to-rule
by its tape player
this is a real person.
British Rail regrets
the cheese shortage
in your sandwich.
This is due to
a points failure.
The steward got
three out of ten.
British Rail regrets.
Tears leak from beneath
the locked doors of staff rooms.
Red-eyed ticket collectors

offer comfort
to stranded passengers.
Angry drivers threaten
to come out in sympathy
with the public.
British Rail regrets.
That's why its members
are permanently dressed in black.
That's why porters stand around
as if in a state of shock.
That's why Passenger Information
is busy
and your call will be answered shortly.

British Rail regrets
that due to the shortage of regrets
there will be a train.

City Sunrise

the smoke
stalks up,
licks the
raw red
underbelly
of morning.

People Who Love

People Who Love

You love her.
But she loves him.
He doesn't care.

So you write poems.
She writes songs.
He doesn't listen.

I love her.
She loves no one.
And no one cares.

I write poems.
I write songs.
You listen.

The world is full
of poems and songs
and people
who love people
who love people
who don't love them.

The Queen of May

Sally I kissed in the classroom
In 1959.
Her hair was like a field of wheat,
Her skin as smooth as pine.

Sally became the Queen of May
And I became her knight.
I stood beside her golden throne,
We both were dressed in white.

We danced around a pole of wood,
Our ribbons crissed and crossed.
We skipped beneath this coloured web
Until the winter frost.

I wonder where she's dancing now,
Her hair as wild as mist,
The girl who was the Queen of May,
The girl that I once kissed?

Ambush

I'm never
falling
tumbling
slipping
or tripping
in love again
I had said,
closing my heart
until further notice.
Little did I realize
that even Love had fallen
foul of technological progress.
Unknown to me, Cupid had
long since traded in
his futile wooden bow
for an automatic rifle.

I'm back again.
Being very good friends.
Trying hard not to notice
the row of holes
    currently appearing
across my chest.

Humanist's Love Poem

Why don't we try loving each other?
(A strange collection of atoms I am).
Feeling this molecular urge for you
– we must chemically react if we can.

One

You make
me whole.
I'm not
half the
man I was.

Declaration of Intent

She said she'd
love me for eternity
but reduced it
to eight months
for good behaviour.
She said we fitted
like a hand in a glove
but then the hot
weather came and such
accessories weren't needed.
She said the future
was ours but the deeds
were made out in
her name.
She said I was
the only one who
understood completely

and then she left me
and said she knew
that I'd understand completely.

One Summer

One summer you
aeroplaned away,
too much money
away for me, and
stayed there for
quite a few
missed embraces.

Before leaving,
you smiled me that
you'd return all of
a mystery moment and
would airletter me
every few breakfasts
in the meantime.
    This
you did, and I thank
you most kissingly.
    I
wish however, that I
could hijackerplane
to the Ignited States
of Neon where I'd
crash land perfectly
in the deserted
airport of your heart.

Letter Bomb

Take care.
It is not
always possible
to detect them
at first glance.
They weigh as much
as circulars
or income tax demands.
Take care.
Normally they start
with a Dear where
a Dearest used to be.
They go on to say
something about not
knowing how to put it.
They put it.
They hope you're not hurt.
You are.
Take care.
Do not plunge the package
into a brine-soaked
handkerchief.
Withdraw.
Call for assistance.

'It's all for the best.'
'Time is a great healer.'

Worship

She worshipped
the ground
I trod on.

Rejected
and full of
jealousy
I dug up
my footprints.

The Examination

You set the first question
    you said
how much are you involved
    with me?
    and I
not being very good
    at science
said I didn't know.
I set the second question
    I said
how do you measure
    an emotion?
    and you
not being very good
    at languages
  smiled at me.

She Was Away for Three Months

Months?
No I never minded
the months.

They looked big
from in front,
but small from
behind.

It was the seconds
I couldn't stand.

Nasty little seconds
that dragged by,
while I discovered
that months
looked big from
in front, but
small from behind.

After Some Thought, a Poem

if i grow a
moustache
for you
will you grow a
ffectionate
for me?

After You'd Gone

No one
like you.
That then
the pleasure.
That now
the pain.

Miss Hart

Your skin
is so soft,
Your cheeks
are so pink.
No teacher
is prettier
Than you are
(I think).

You teach me
mathematics.
You help me
to spell.
I learn about
lipstick
And perfume
as well.

I'm only
a child
And you're
twenty-two
But I love you
Miss Hart.
I honestly do.

I Don't Like Girls

I don't like girls. Not me.
Girls are wet.
Girls play girls' games.
I want to go out
with the boys.
Snogging's daft.
I saw it on telly.
I'll never snog a girl.
Not me.

I like some girls.
Some girls are fun.
Some girls are like boys.
They play good games.
You can have a girl
who is your friend,
but that doesn't mean
that she's your *girlfriend*.
Girlfriends are silly.

I quite like girls.
They make me feel funny inside.
It's a nice sort of funny, though.
I dreamed about a girl once.
I don't think girls
really like boys.
Girls only play with girls.

I really like girls.
Girls are great.
They wear skirts.
Snogging's fantastic.
You can play games
that make you feel
funny inside.
I think girls really like me.

I like this girl.
She's great.
When I'm with her
the world falls away.
We think the same thoughts.
We want to be with each other
to the end of the world.

I don't like girls. Not me.
Girls are wet.
They wear skirts.
Girls talk girls' talk.
I want to go out with the lads.
Romance is daft.
They see it all on telly.
You'll never catch me
going all soft.
Not me.

Voices

I love you.
Do you?
I love you.
I'm glad.
I love you.
I know you do.
I love you.
Thank you.
Do you love me?
Who couldn't?
Do you love me?
Doesn't it show?
Do you love me?
I admire you.
Do you love me?
There's no one else.
I love you.
I remember.

Write a Poem for Me

Write a poem for me, she said.
You wrote one for Mary
Who was all airy-fairy,
And you wrote one for Jenny and Lynne.
You wrote such nice words
For all your old birds,
Why can't you write something for me?

Write a poem for you? I said.
You're beyond all compare,
It would hardly be fair.
It would be like describing the dew.
The words don't exist
For beauty like this.
I couldn't write something for you.

Write a poem for me, she said.
It looks a bit rough,
When you wrote all that stuff
For Linda and for Irene and Sue,
To not be inspired
By the one you admire.
I think it's the least you could do.

Write a poem for you? I said.
They all gave me such grief.
I wrote them more for relief.
I was trying to escape from the pain.
But you bring me such bliss
My poem is a kiss.
I couldn't write love verse again.

Write a poem for me, she said.
I shall give you a start.
You can use the word heart,
Then you can talk about how much you care.
'Without me you're lost.'
'An ocean that's tossed.'
One verse and you'd almost be there.

Write a poem for you? I said.
'My heart is an ocean
You stir my emotion
I am tossed like a lettuce in spring
For you do I care
I'm lost in your hair.'
Would this be the right kind of thing?

I knew you could do it, she said.
I'll keep it for ever.
You're so very clever.
You've made me immortal today.
It didn't take hours,
Lasts longer than flowers,
And has none of the fat of Milk Tray.

I Am on the Kids' Side

I Am on the Kids' Side

I am on the kids' side
in the war against adults.
I don't want to stand still.
I don't want to sit still.
I don't want to be quiet.
I believe that strangers
are for staring at,
bags are for looking into,
paper is for scribbling on.
I want to know Why.
I want to know How.
I wonder What If.
I am on the kids' side
in the war against tedium.
I'm for going home
when stores get packed.
I'm for sleeping in
when parties get dull.
I'm for kicking stones
when conversation sags.
I'm for making noises.
I'm for playing jokes –
especially in life's
more Serious Bits.
I am on the kids' side.
See my sneaky grin,

watch me dance, see me run.
Spit on the carpet, rub it in,
pick my nose in public,
play rock stars in the mirror.
I am on the kids' side.
I want to know why we're not moving.
I'm fed up. I want to go out.
What's that? Can I have one?
It isn't fair. Who's that man?
It wasn't me, I was pushed.
When are we going to go?
I am on the kids' side
putting fun back into words.
Ink pink pen and ink
you go out because you stink.
Stephen Turner is a burner,
urner, murner, purner.
Stephen, weven, peven,
reven, teven, Turnip Top.
I am on the kids' side
in the war against apathy.
Mum, I want to do something.
It must be my turn next.
When can we go out?
I am on the kids' side
and when I grow up,
I want to be a boy.

When Grandad Comes to Stay

We must be well-behaved
When Grandad comes to stay
No sliding down the staircase
Until he goes away
No running in the hall
Or playing games like chase
We have to clean our ears
And keep a well-scrubbed face.

We have to be so quiet
When Grandad's in his chair
We have to sneak around
As if we're hardly there
We can't play our CDs
Or punch each other's heads
We have to clean our rooms
And make up our own beds.

We need to be polite
When Grandad comes to us
No burping during mealtimes
Or letting slip a cuss
We must say please and thank you
And could you pass the cup
Then Grandad will believe that
We've all been well brought up.

Ten Things Mums Never Say

1. Keep your mouth open when you eat,
   then you'll be able to talk at the same time.

2. Jump down the stairs.
   It's quicker than walking.

3. Don't eat all your vegetables.
   You won't have enough room for your sweets.

4. It's too early for bed.
   Stay up and watch more television.

5. Be rude to your teachers.
   It would be dishonest to be polite.

6. By all means walk on the furniture.
   It's already badly scratched.

7. Don't brush your teeth.
   They'll only get dirty again.

8. It's not your fault that your pocket money
   only lasts for a day.

9. Wipe your feet on the sofas.
   That's what they're there for.

10. I was far worse behaved than you
    when I was young.

Questions

Do you need to go to the toilet
when you are dead?
Does God grow old?

Life is full
of unanswered questions
when you are five years old,
and late for school.

Dad, You're Not Funny

A few of my mates
Come around to our place
And you're at the door
With a grin on your face.
You know that I know
You're a really good bloke,
But I'll curl up and die
If you tell us a joke.

We don't want to hear
About your days at school,
We don't want to watch
You try to be cool.
We don't want to know
How the world used to be.
We don't want to see
Those videos of me.

We don't want to laugh
At your riddles and rhymes,
At musty old tales
We've heard fifty times.
We don't want a quiz
Where we have to compete,
We don't want to guess
Why the hen crossed the street.

Please don't perform
That ridiculous dance
Like you did on the night
We went out in France.
Don't do impressions
Of pop stars on drugs.
Whatever you do
Don't swamp me with hugs.

So Dad, don't come in,
Your jokes are so dated
I often pretend
That we're not related.
I'd pay you to hide
If I had my own money
The simple truth is –
Dad, you're not funny.

Rebecca's Father

Rebecca's father
knows everything
(or so she
told my son).

Rebecca knows
that her father
knows everything
because he told her.

And he should know.
He knows everything.

The Day I Fell Down the Toilet

The day I fell down the toilet
Is a day I'll never forget,
One moment I was in comfort,
The next I was helpless and wet.

My feet tipped up to the ceiling,
My body collapsed in the bowl,
In haste I grabbed at the handle
And found myself flushed down a hole.

One wave goodbye to the bathroom
And I was lost in the sewer,
Travelling tunnels and caverns
On a raft made out of manure.

Then came the washing-up water
With bits of spaghetti and peas,
The filth from a local factory
And an undiscovered disease.

Drifting along in the darkness,
There was nothing to do but wait.
What would I say to my mum now?
What was it that made me so late?

Suddenly it was all over,
From the end of a pipe I shot
Into a part of the ocean
Where the rubbish was sent to rot.

Glad to escape from the tunnel
To leave all pollution behind,
I found a nice spot on the beach,
Then started to bathe and unwind.

But bad things began to pursue me,
They stuck to my feet and my hand,
Wreckage was surfing the wave tops
And oil lay around on the sand.

I figured the sewer was safer
For no one said sewers were clean,
I found the pipe that I came from
And waded my way back upstream.

When I got home I was shattered,
I was filthy, ragged and wet,
Rattling the bathroom door was Dad
Saying, 'You off that toilet yet?'

Noise

When I play
my records
(at full volume,
in stereo)
I have to
close all
the windows.

I can't stand
the noise
of the birds
outside
in the trees.

In My Day

In my day
we got up at dawn,
made our own beds,
cooked our breakfasts,
walked to school,
worked hard,
didn't talk in class,
walked home,
enjoyed our homework,
ate all our food,
washed our plates
and went to bed early.
And told lies.

Who's a Lovely Girl?

Well, who's a lovely girl then?
(Not me, you stupid bat.)
And who's got shiny hair then?
(You'd think I was the cat.)

You're so much like your mummy.
(I think I'm just like me.)
With little bits of grandma.
(I have to disagree.)

And, wow, you have grown taller!
(That's what we humans do.)
And who's a clever girl then?
(Obviously not you.)

Assembly

We assemble.
That's why it's called
assembly.
We sit cross-legged.
The area of the bottom
multiplied by the number of pupils
is greater than the area
of the hall floor.
We squiggle, we squeeze,
we squash, we squabble.
Jamie is asked to stay behind.
Behind is another word for bottom.
Miss walks on the stage.
So does Miss, Miss, Sir,
Miss, Sir, Miss, Miss and
Miss.

We have a talk about being good.
It is good to be good.
It is bad to be bad.
We will all be good.
We sing a song about trees.
The bone in my bottom
cuts into the floorboards.
I'm not worried about the floorboards.
Miss reads out the notices
but nobody notices.
We stand up.
I pull my bottom bone
out of the floorboards.
We line up like soldiers,
like prisoners, like refugees.

We file out
in a sensible manner.
The hall is now empty.
Except for Jamie.

The Notices

Here are the notices:

It has come to my attention
that Dumpty, in the green class,
has been climbing the wall.
This is against school rules.
If he's not careful, he'll fall.

The same applies to the hill.
Get your water from the tap,
not the well.
It's a dangerous place.
Ask Jack. Ask Jill.

Food is not to be eaten in class.
This includes Christmas pie
in the corner; take note, Jack Horner.
The tuffet, as I have stressed,
is still out of bounds.

Speaking of food brings me
to school dinners.
If, like Jack Sprat, you are on
a special diet, please inform
Mrs Hubbard in the canteen.
Low-fat meals are now available.

Items of cutlery have been disappearing.
I want this to stop.
No more excuses like:
'I didn't steal that spoon –
the dish ran away with it.'
It just doesn't wash.

There will be a parents' evening
next Wednesday in the main hall.
The title of the lecture is 'Cat Rescue'
and the speaker will be Tommy Stout.
Music will be performed by
Little Boy Blue and the King Cole Fiddlers.

Finally, a word about dress.
The following items are not
part of the school uniform:
dusty skirts, rabbit skin,
trousers with knee buckles,
nightgowns. With this in mind,
would the following please stay behind:
Shaftoe, Flinders, Bunting, Winkie.

The Teacher's Gift

(Margarette Nicholson, 1909–85)

Every time I tell the time
Or work out ten times two,
I open up a precious gift
Bequeathed to me by you.

You gave me names and numbers.
You taught me how to spell.
You told me how to hold a pen
And how to write as well.

You showed me how to read aloud
From books of red and blue.
You filled my head with goats and trolls
And tinderboxes too.

You planted seeds inside me
But did not see them grow.
A bell rings at the end of school
We pack our bags and go.

These words I scrawl on paper,
This shape upon my tongue,
Is made from things you gave to me
Way back when I was young.

You're It!

(For Mark)

I make castles
You be ghost.
I kick football
You be post.
I play teacher
You be taught.
I play crime squad
You be caught.

I play tag chase
You be it.
I play kick box
You be hit.
I play hero
You be man.
I play film star
You play fan.

I play farmer
You be pig.
I play doctor
You be sick.
I play leader
You be led.
I play soldier
You play dead.

Best Friends

Best friends tell you secrets
Best friends always play
Best friends send you postcards
When they go away.

Best friends guess your thinking
Best friends read your eyes
Best friends notice right away
If you're telling lies.

Best friends say they're sorry
Best friends say they care
Best friends may be absent
But they're always there.

Stuck at Seventeen (Rock 'n' Roll Poem)

Hey mum I'm all grown up
Yet I feel like a kid
Must be something I ate
Or something that you did
I'm going on thirty
And I'm stuck at seventeen
Should be into grey suits
And I'm still wearing jeans

You said that rock 'n' roll
Was an adolescent phase
That sprung up like a spot
And disappeared in days
You said I'd see sense
Then turn into a man
Try Tchaikovsky
Throw my records in the can

But I'm all grown up and I'm stuck at seventeen
You'll never make me different from the way I've
    always been
I'm all grown up and I'm stuck at seventeen
I'm an innocent delinquent and a rock 'n' rolling being

You showed me winklepickers
And the cramping of the toes
Losses of employment
Through the colour of me clothes
Possible delinquency
By wearing tapered jeans
Effects of rock 'n' roll
Upon impressionable teens

You really did your best
To try and make me get well
With those sensible shoes
And the tubes of Trugel
With the nice sons of friends
And some hymns with a beat
And modern brown sandals
To give me healthy feet.

But I'm all grown up and I'm stuck at seventeen
You'll never make me different from the way I've
   always been
I'm all grown up and I'm stuck at seventeen
I'm an innocent delinquent and a rock 'n' rolling being

But nothin' really worked
I'm in a leather jacket
I tried wearin' ties but
My neck couldn't hack it
Don't wait for Steve mother
He's never gonna grow
He's gonna be like Johnny
And just Go, Go, Go.

Wait

These are
the good
old days.

Just wait
and see.

I Don't Believe in Air

I Don't Believe in Air

I don't believe in air.
No one has ever seen it.
No one has ever felt it
between finger and thumb.
Converts talk about
tasting the air
and smelling the air,
but there's always another explanation;
the nearby sea, a factory's pipes,
a pile of fresh manure.
It's not the so-called air
that smells.

Scientists have complete faith
in this air.
They say that it upholds
and sustains our world.
Take away the air, they argue,
and we'd go too.
Meteorologists attribute
signs and wonders to the air;
people thrown to the ground,
trees uprooted, the landscape rearranged.

It sounds like superstition to me.
If there is air,
who made it?
Where does it all go?
Why doesn't it show itself
just one time for proof?

Friends ask me why windows rattle
and hair goes awry,
but I don't believe in air.
I don't believe in air.
Air is just another word
for something that's not there.

Disney World USA

I don't need to go to the jungle
For I've been on the Jungle Ride
I know what it's like to be snapped at
To look in a crocodile's eye
I've felt the heat of the midday sun
Sailed under a waterfall
I don't need to go to the jungle
I don't need to go there at all.

I don't need to climb up a mountain
After riding the Thunder train
I lost my life a hundred times
And then I went back there again
I rode the dangerous northern face
Where the rocks and boulders fall
I don't need to climb up a mountain
I don't need to climb one at all.

I don't need to go to New Orleans –
A riverboat crosses the lake
There's always a bowl of Gumbo soup
Traditional jazz is on tape
You can see the architecture's French
You can join in the Mardi Gras
I don't need to go to New Orleans
I don't need to go that far.

I don't need to wander round the world
For the world has travelled to me
We did China, France and Mexico
Then popped into England for tea
I've eaten every national dish
And bought up their souvenirs
I don't need to wander round the world
I don't need to move from here.

I don't need to leave the atmosphere
I've already been to the moon
I've cruised around the galaxy
And come back the same afternoon
Flying along at the speed of light
While making a screaming sound
I don't need to leave the atmosphere
I don't need to leave the ground.

I don't need to die and rise again
When heaven has come to the earth
There is no sin or sadness here
It's like having a second birth
I gave my burdens to Mickey Mouse
And he pardoned me with a kiss
I don't need to die and rise again
I'm perfectly happy with this.

Five Hundred Million Pounds

The Earl of Grosvenor
has five hundred million pounds.
He is honeymooning in Hawaii.
He has five hundred million pounds
and he still has to honeymoon
in the world.
He has married Natalia.
She is not my sort of girl.
Five hundred million pounds
and he marries someone
who is not my sort of girl.
The Earl of Grosvenor
carries a black case
in his right hand.
Five hundred million pounds
and he still has to carry
a black case in his right hand.
It is probably heavy.
He will probably sweat.
Damp patches will form
beneath his arms
as if he was a construction worker
or an unemployed gentleman
carrying a black case.
I expect his shoes hurt sometimes.
I expect he forgets his handkerchief.
I expect he wonders whether Natalia
really loves him.
I expect he wonders what it would be like
to have only four hundred and fifty
million pounds.
The Earl of Grosvenor takes off.

He wonders whether the engines will catch fire.
He knows you can't pay engines off.
He knows that the ocean is indifferent to millionaires.
Five hours in the air and he is restless.
Five hundred million pounds and he is restless.

Creed

We believe in Freud and Darwin.
We believe everything is OK
as long as we don't hurt anyone,
to the best of our definition of hurt,
and to the best of our knowledge.

We believe in sex before, during,
and after marriage.
We believe in the therapy of sin.
We believe that adultery can be helpful.
We believe that taboos are taboo.

We believe that everything's getting better
despite evidence to the contrary.
The evidence must be investigated.
You can prove anything with evidence.

We believe there's something in horoscopes,
UFOs and bent spoons;
Jesus was a good man just like Buddha,
Mohammed and ourselves.
He was a good moral teacher, although we think
his good morals were bad.

We believe that all religions are basically the same,
at least the one that we read about was.
They all believe in love and goodness.
They only differ on matters of
creation sin heaven hell God and salvation.

We believe that after death comes The Nothing
because when you ask the dead what happens
they say Nothing.
If death is not the end, if the dead have lied,
then it's compulsory heaven for all
excepting perhaps Hitler, Stalin and Genghis Khan.

We believe in the most recent survey.
What's selected is average.
What's average is normal.
What's normal is good.

We believe in total disarmament.
We believe there are direct links between
warfare and bloodshed.
The goodies should beat their guns into tractors
and the baddies will be sure to follow.

We believe that man is essentially good.
It's only his behaviour that lets him down.
This is the fault of society.
Society is the fault of conditions.
Conditions are the fault of society.

We believe that each man must find the truth
that is right for him.
Reality will adapt accordingly.
The universe will readjust. History will alter.
We believe that there is no absolute truth
excepting the truth that there is no absolute truth.

We believe in the rejection of creeds.

Everything

Looks aren't everything.
Luxury's not everything.
Money's not everything.
Health is not everything.
Success is not everything.
Happiness is not everything.
Even everything is not everything.
There's more to life than everything.

Beaten But Not Lost

(For Irina Ratushinskaya)

We beat her
and she lost weight.
She lost blood.
She lost consciousness.

But she never lost hope.
She never lost poetry.
And she was never lost.

You must have to beat real hard
to get the God
out of these people;
to still the noise of heaven
in their hearts.

Death Sex Religion and Politics

I'm afraid we don't talk about death here,
not while drinking tea.
Death is a private matter.
It's up to the individual.
Thinking about it won't make it any easier.
You can worry yourself to death
but not back again.
Sex is a private matter too.
People shouldn't have problems.
I learned everything I needed through jokes at school.
Thinking about it doesn't make it any easier.
Sex is another thing we don't talk about.
Religion? Well, each man to his own, I say.
It's bad manners to argue religion.
They all lead to God.
There's no difference between Buddhism
and frog worship.
I learned all I need to know about religion at school.
You can worry yourself to death but not to heaven.
I'm afraid we don't discuss politics here.
Politics is a private matter
like sex and death.
Like all religions, all politicians are the same.
They all lead to death.
I learned all that I need to know about knowing
at school.

'Religion is the Opium of the People'

This opium is dangerous.
Colourless, odourless,
and smuggled in the heart,
nevertheless this opium
is dangerous.
It changes people,
it will turn our children into enemies.
This opium makes them mad.
They start seeing things,
imagining the world big with spirit,
long with heaven.
They start to fantasize,
imagine there's more than meets the eye.
This opium makes them joyous.
You can tell if they have this opium.
Listen for their singing,
look closely in their eyes,
hear them whisper in the air.
They lose all interest
in making money
or conquering the world.
They lose all interest in us
when they discover this opium.
We have them registered now.
They are eighty per cent of us.
We shall watch them closely.
The public must not be infected.

How to Hide Jesus

There are people after Jesus.
They have seen the signs.
Quick, let's hide Him.
Let's think; carpenter,
    fishermen's friend,
    disturber of religious comfort.
Let's award Him a degree in theology,
a purple cassock
and a position of respect.
They'll never think of looking here.
Let's think;
    His dialect may betray Him,
    His tongue is of the masses.
Let's teach Him Latin
and seventeenth-century English,
they'll never think of listening in.
Let's think;
    humble
    Man Of Sorrows,
nowhere to lay His head.
We'll build a house for Him,
somewhere away from the poor.
We'll fill it with brass and silence.
It's sure to throw them off.

There are people after Jesus.
Quick, let's hide Him.

The Prophet

You didn't stone the prophet.
The odd joke or two maybe.
Impersonations, a cartoon.
A hint of 'trouble in the brain'.
But you didn't stone him,
there are no bruises, no breaks.
You didn't stone the prophet.
He's alive and walking.
Not on TV much, not on radio,
but in the countryside, somewhere.
(I saw a photograph.)
You didn't stone the prophet.
But then look at the trouble_
you've had with martyrs.
Everyone wants to hear them.
The dead are so hard to shut up.
You didn't stone the prophet.
You just told us that he had problems.
Nothing that a prostitute
or a psychiatrist couldn't cure.
He's too young or old,
too fascist or socialist.
No, you didn't stone the prophet.
You gave him the microphone
every now and then
and supplied us with experts
to add some perspective.
The official view is
        Don't Panic.
No, you didn't stone the prophet.
You said there were crazies like him
around in ancient Rome

but Italy survives.
The official view was
    Don't Panic.
You didn't stone the prophet.
You didn't even censor him.
You didn't put him in prison.
You just put him in perspective.

Churchotheque

They're charging £5.90
for colour posters of their
supersaints.
They're asking for 10,000
to renovate the bishop.
The public are invited
to inspect the stained glass
strip cartoons,
light a candle for the builders
and sing hosannas
to the architect.
You can buy a booklet of its
history and an ashtray with a
picture, before guiding your
conscience past the begging
money boxes.
They have a concert there on
Tuesdays, a garden fête each
month, as well as the obligatory
service or two.
And, oh yes, I'm glad that you
asked about God.
He was made redundant in their
latest promotional campaign.
The moving finger of public
opinion wrote His obituary
on the wall.
Jesus was evicted for the
operatic society to rehearse.
Now, you'll find Him in the
houses if you care to take a
look. You'll hear Him in the

streets if you get a chance
to listen.
There's not enough room in
the churchotheque.
It's Christmas all over again.

7/8 of the Truth and Nothing but the Truth

If you are sitting comfortably
I suspect I am not giving you
the truth.
I am leaving you two poems
short of disagreement
so that you can remark upon
the likeness of our minds.
I am being kind.
I am giving you truth
in linctus form – strawberry flavour.
I am being unkind.
I am ignoring the correct dosage.

I want to be liked.
That's my trouble.
I want to be agreed with.
I know you all like strawberry,
I quite like it myself.
It's nothing but the truth
but it's not the whole truth.

No one admires the whole truth.
No one ever applauds.
It takes things too far.
It's nice but where would
you put it?
People who neglect the strawberry
flavouring, do not get asked back.
They get put in their place,
with nails if necessary.

Questions, Questions

I'm always asking questions
But no one seems to know.
The sky, where does it end?
The wind, where does it go?

What keeps the stars from falling,
What holds the moon above?
Do dogs have dreams and nightmares,
Do rabbits fall in love?

Does time go on for ever,
And when did time begin?
Did God make all from nothing
And, if so, who made him?

I'm always asking questions
But no one seems to know.
Where do these puzzles come from?
Where do the answers go?

I Wish I Could Believe

'I wish I could believe,' you say,
Although that's not strictly true.
You have enough muscle and brain,
It's finding something that's *you*.
Religion should be cut to fit,
You think. It should stretch and bend.
Why should you 'take up your cross'
If the grain of wood won't blend?

'I'd love a faith like yours,' you say,
Although that's not strictly true.
Your faith is like mine in a way,
But it all folds back on you.
You believe in yourself, you said.
You'll eyeball God if he's there.
This stuff about heaven and hell –
Does anyone really care?

'Perhaps one day I will,' you say,
And although this could be true,
I think it's one of those things
You'll never get round to do,
Like the friend you really must see,
The novel that burns in your soul,
There's a sudden interruption
As soil is tossed down a hole.

Truth

There's no
such thing
as truth.

No.
Not even
    this.

Careful How You Pray

Careful How You Pray

Careful how you pray now.
You pray justice
come rollin' down
like a mighty river
and it might just come rollin'.
Might come rollin'
down your street.
Might come beatin'
up your walls.
Might come lickin'
'neath your door.

Might get wet.
Might drown.

Spiritus

I used to think of you
as a symphony
neatly structured,
full of no surprises.
Now I see you as
a saxophone solo
blowing wildly
into the night,
a tongue of fire,
flicking in unrepeated
    patterns.

Here Am I

This is my flesh.
I give it to you.
These are my thoughts,
and this is my work.
Here are my faults.
Here is the fear
I discuss with myself.
Here are my good jokes,
here are my bad ones.
The flesh is falling apart,
it will have to do.
The thoughts are uncontrollable
some of them hate each other.

Here is my sweat,
and my decay,
the face only mirrors see.
This is my love
and my lack of love.
Here is my laughter.
Here are the years.
Here am I.

Well Done

You said you'd never leave me.
Never forsake me.
But I haven't heard you around
these parts for a month or so.
Do you still get my messages
tossed up each day?
Can you hear my anguish?
I know you send postcards
through trees and clouds.
I know that your smile
is somehow in every smile.
I read your letters.
I listen to your songs.
But I long for that
personal touch.
I want that pat on the back,
that whisper in the ear,
that look in the eye.
I want to hear you say,
'Well done.'

The God Letters

The Lord God says:
'Share your bread
with the hungry,
bring the homeless poor
into your house,
cover the naked.'

Dear Lord God,
We have got
new carpets,
so this will
not be possible.

Just One More Time

Lead me into temptation
just one more time.
Lead me up close
through circumstances
beyond my control.
Lead me then leave me.
Deliver me from escape,
increase my ignorance,
limit my will.
Make me the victim of
a victim-less crime.
Leave me 'til sin
is the only way out,
give me a taste of
what to avoid.
Leave me 'til it's
your fault
yet guilt floods me
like a chill.
Then lead me back
into temptation,
just one more time.

Thank You

Thank you for the blanket
that spreads on my bed
Thank you for the pillow
that cradles my head
Thank you for the darkness
that rolls through the skies
Thank you for the tiredness
that closes my eyes.

Thank you for the windows
that keep out the storm
Thank you for the heating
that helps me stay warm
Thank you for the four walls
that make up my room
Thank you for the cold light
that falls from the moon.

Thank you for the loved ones
who sleep in this place
Thank you for the memories
that light up my face
Thank you for the silence
that comes with the night
Thank you for the feeling
that everything's right.

The Jogger's Prayer

From apple skins keep me I pray
And all things touched by deadly spray
May additives be subtracted
Spare me all that's radioactive

Give me eggs of deepest yellow
Free of dust and salmonella
Then bless my heart with margarine
And coffee beans with no caffeine

Remove all chemicals from fish
Let not an oil slick smear my dish
And should I lie beneath the sun
Ban deadly rays before they come

Guide me beside a kitchen sink
With waters cleansed of lead and zinc
Shield me from the central heating
Double glazing, careless eating

Divine the air meant for my lungs
And filter any dirt that comes
Preserve my tubes and keep them clean
Deliver me from nicotine

Then when I jog please bless my knees
Keep me from Legionnaire's disease
Hold my bowels and discs in place
Don't let me trip and gash my face

Above all bring me peace of mind
When wholefood gets too hard to find
And experts can't agree what's best
And staying healthy leads to stress.

Prayer

Fell fast asleep
While saying a prayer.
When I woke up
Found God was still there.

Psalm

Not my works
    but your work
Not my perfection
    but yours
Not my grasp
    but your grip
Not my completeness
    but yours.

Not my strength
    but your strength
Not my honesty
    but yours
Not my trust
    but your truth
Not my will be done
    but yours.

Who Made the World?

Who Made the World?

Who was it who made the world, Sir?
A bang brought creation about.
Who set off the explosion, Sir?
I don't know. They're still finding out.

Did this big bang make you deaf, Sir?
It happened a long time ago.
How do you know it happened, Sir?
A man in a book told me so.

Who was the man in the book, Sir?
A man who looked up in the sky.
How do you know that he knew, Sir?
Because I believe him, that's why.

Who was it who made me and you, Sir?
A creature crept out of the sea.
Who was it who made the creature, Sir?
The creature just happened to be.

Why did it creep from the sea, Sir?
It thought it was time for a change.
How did it grow arms and legs, Sir?
I know, it sounds awfully strange.

Where do we go when we die, Sir?
Don't know, but I'm sure that it's great.
Who was it who made the place great, Sir?
No talking now children, it's late.

In the Beginning

God said WORLD
and the world spun round,
God said LIGHT
and the light beamed down,
God said LAND
and the sea rolled back,
God said NIGHT
and the sky went black.

God said LEAF
and the shoot pushed through,
God said FIN
and the first fish grew,
God said BEAK
and the big bird soared,
God said FUR
and the jungle roared.

God said SKIN
and the man breathed air,
God said BONE
and the girl stood there,
God said GOOD
and the world was great,
God said REST
and they all slept late.

The Naming of the Animals

What would you call this animal, Adam?
He's proud and he prowls and he roars,
He's stronger than anyone else I made,
His coat is the colour of straw.

What would you call this animal, Adam?
Her neck stretches up to the trees,
She has four legs as skinny as sticks
And four very knobbly knees.

What would you call this animal, Adam,
With a tube instead of a nose?
His ears are like clothes on a washing line
And he hurrumphs wherever he goes.

What would you call this animal, Adam?
Her skin is as tough as old rope,
A horn sticks up on the end of her nose
And mud is her favourite soap.

What would you call this animal, Adam?
He swoops from the sky for his lunch,
He knits his own house from branches and leaves
And swallows a mouse with a crunch.

What would you call this person, Adam?
I want her to be your best friend.
Make sure you love her with all of your heart
And stay by her side 'til the end.

Adam's Story of Bedtime

It was the middle of the night.
I felt a dig in my ribs,
but thought nothing of it.
Rolled over and dreamed
of vegetation and rivers.

Got up. Washed my face.
Noticed a thin red line
running across my side.
It wasn't there the day before
or the day before that.

I was breathing in and out,
feeling my bones,
when I saw myself
walking towards me.

It was like looking in water
except the hips were different,
the chest, the hair.

The lips parted.
Mine didn't.
'Have you lost something?'
she asked.
'Loneliness,'
I said.

The Serpent

The serpent is more subtle.
He is more subtle
than a rhinoceros
who cannot slither up unsuspectingly.
He is more subtle
than a lion
who cannot swing from branches.
He is more subtle
than a terrapin,
   a goat,
more subtle than truth.
You think he is a stick
until you collect him
for firewood.
You think he is a leaf
until he bends down
to kiss.
You think he is a stone,
   a tree,
   a good idea,
   your true self.
The serpent has more beauty.
He amazes you with his colour
which speaks with the sun.
He amazes you with his grace.
If you have not been told,
you will want to take him in your hand,
you will want to take him home.

What Am I?

This bow is made of sunshine
This bow is made of rain
This bow is many-coloured
This bow says not again.

My Dad

My dad's bigger than your dad.
My dad's as tall as the moon,
as strong as the wind,
as wide as the sky.
You should see my dad!
He's got stars in his fists.
He bends rainbows on his knee.
When he breathes, clouds move.

He's good is my dad.
You can't scare him with the dark.
You can't scare him with guns or sticks.
He makes bullies say sorry
just by staring.
Big green monsters
fall asleep on his lap.
Ghosts start haunting each other.

My dad's been everywhere
but he says he likes the world.
Earth people are fun, he says.
My dad knows more than teacher.
He knows everything.
He knows what you're thinking,
even when you try to trick him
by thinking something else.
If you tell a lie
my dad says he can tell
by the look on your face.

My dad's the best dad ever.
I say I love him
a million times a million
times a million times a million trillion.
My dad says he loves me
a billion trillion times more than that.

My dad likes to love.
My dad made the world.

Christmas

We'll hang up our stockings
We always do that.
And I'll wake up early
I always do that.
There'll be a notebook and pen
I always get that.
And a chocolate bar
I always eat that.

Then downstairs for breakfast
I always leave that.
We stand by the front room
We always do that.
Then Dad says, 'Come in'
He always says that.
And we sit with our presents
We always do that.

Then there's tearing and scrunching
I always hear that.
We say, 'Just what I wanted'
We always say that.
Then turkey for dinner
We always have that.
And mince pies for tea
We always eat that.

The thing about Christmas
I always think that
Is that it stays the same
Always like that.
And that's why I love it
I love it like that.
Everything else changes
But we always do that.

Christmas is Really for the Children

Christmas is really
for the children.
Especially for children
who like animals, stables,
stars and babies wrapped
in swaddling clothes.
Then there are wise men,
kings in fine robes,
humble shepherds and a
hint of rich perfume.

Easter is not really
for the children
unless accompanied by
a cream-filled egg.
It has whips, blood, nails,
a spear and allegations
of body-snatching.
It involves politics, God
and the sins of the world.
It is not good for people
of a nervous disposition.
They would do better to
think on rabbits, chickens
and the first snowdrop
of spring.

Or they'd do better to
wait for a re-run of
Christmas without asking
too many questions about
what Jesus did when he grew up
or whether there's any connection.

Disciples

They threw down their nets
and they followed Him.
There was no time to
calculate profit or loss.
There was no time to
call home for a second opinion.
It seemed like absolute madness.
It seemed like death.
But it was a wise madness,
a necessary death.
The old faith dropped
and sank beneath waves.
The new faith walked on water,
beckoning on to Jerusalem
and the dry hills around.

The Cast of Christmas Reassembles for Easter

Take the wise men to the Emperor's palace.
Wash their hands in water.
Get them to say something about truth.
Does anyone know any good Jewish jokes?
The one about the carpenter
who thought he was a King?
The one about the Saviour
who couldn't save himself?
The shepherds should stand with the chorus.
They have a big production number –
'Barabbas, We Love You Baby'.
Mary? She can move to the front.
We have a special section reserved
for family and close friends.
Tell her that we had to cut the manger up.
We needed the wood for something else.
The star I'm afraid I can't use.
There are no stars in this show.
The sky turns black with sorrow.
The earth shakes with terror.
Hold on to the frankincense.
We'll need that for the garden scene.
Angels? He could do with some angels.
Avenging angels.
Merciful angels.
He could really do with some angels.
Baby Jesus.
Step this way please.
My! How you've grown!

Poem for Easter

Tell me:
What came first
Easter or the egg?
Crucifixion
    or daffodils?
Three days in a tomb
    or four days
in Paris?
    (returning
Bank Holiday Monday).

When is a door
not a door?
When it is rolled away.
When is a body
not a body?
When it is a risen.

Question.
Why was it the Saviour
rode on the cross?
Answer.
To get us
to the other side.

Behold I stand.
Behold I stand and what?
Behold I stand at the door and

knock knock.

The Crucifixion

You were one with the Father.
Then the Father turned his back on you.
You felt forsaken,
hanging there between heaven's thunder
and the spittle of earth.

For that moment you belonged nowhere.
You were love, cut off from love;
truth nailed down by lies.
You must have wanted to explode, to disintegrate,
to disappear into a void.
But that was forbidden.
And that was the test.

Your blood burst through your skin
and ran down like sweat.
Your sweat ran cold
and drained into your heart.
The universe vibrated with your pain.
The sun went blind with grief.
The earth shivered with shock.
History was torn in two.

I stood at a distance,
my collar turned up;
a criminal witnessing
a wrongful arrest.

The Nail Man

Which one was it
who held the nails
and then hammered them
into place?

Did he hit them
out of anger,
or a simple
sense of duty?

Was it a job
that had to be done,
or a good day's work
in the open air?

And when they
slid past bone
and bit into wood,
was it like all the others,
or did history
shudder a little
beneath the head
of that hammer?

Was he still there,
packing away his tools,
when *It is finished*
was uttered to the throng,
or was he at home
washing his hands
and getting ready
for the night?

Will he be
among the forgiven
on the Day of Days,
his sin having been skewered
by his own savage spike?

The Morning That Death Was Killed

I woke in a place that was dark
The air was spicy and still
I was bandaged from head to foot
The morning that death was killed.

I rose from a mattress of stone
I folded my clothes on the sill
I heard the door rolling open
The morning that death was killed.

I walked alone in the garden
The birds in the branches trilled
It felt like a new beginning
The morning that death was killed.

Mary, she came there to find me
Peter with wonder was filled
And John came running and jumping
The morning that death was killed.

My friends were lost in amazement
My father, I knew, was thrilled
Things were never the same again
After the morning that death was killed.

Index of First Lines

Listed below are Steve Turner's previously published collections of poetry:

Tonight We Will Fake Love, 1974
Nice and Nasty, 1980
Up to Date (*UD*), 1983 (This included the collections above)
King of Twist (*KT*), 1992
The Day I Fell Down the Toilet (*DFDT*), 1996
Dad, You're Not Funny (*DYNF*), 1999
The Moon Has Got His Pants On (*MP*), 2001